BLACK TRAILBLAZERS IN SPORTS

WILMA RUDOLPH

by David Lee Morgan Jr.

FOCUS READERS

NAVIGATOR

WWW.FOCUSREADERS.COM

Focus Readers is distributed by North Star Editions:
sales@northstareditions.com | 888-417-0195

Produced for Focus Readers by Red Line Editorial.

Photographs ©: AP Images, cover, 1, 10–11, 16–17, 24; Jerry Cooke/Corbis Historical/Getty Images, 4–5; Bettmann/Getty Images, 6, 9, 13, 15, 19, 22–23, 26; Corbis Historical/Getty Images, 21; Red Line Editorial, 29

Library of Congress Cataloging-in-Publication Data
Names: Morgan, David Lee, author.
Title: Wilma Rudolph / by David Lee Morgan, Jr.
Description: Mendota Heights, MN: Focus Readers, [2025] | Series: Black trailblazers in sports | Includes bibliographical references and index. | Audience: Grades 4-6
Identifiers: LCCN 2023054177 (print) | LCCN 2023054178 (ebook) | ISBN 9798889982128 (hardcover) | ISBN 9798889982685 (paperback) | ISBN 9798889983750 (pdf) | ISBN 9798889983248 (ebook)
Subjects: LCSH: Rudolph, Wilma, 1940-1994--Juvenile literature. | African American women sprinters--United States--Juvenile literature. | African American track and field athletes--Tennessee--Biography--Juvenile literature. | Women athletes with disabilities--United States--Juvenile literature. | Tennessee State University--Sports--History--Juvenile literature. | African American women Olympic athletes--Tennessee--Biography--Juvenile literature. | Olympic Games (16th : 1956 : Melbourne, Vic.)--Juvenile literature. | Olympic Games (17th : 1960 : Rome, Italy)--Juvenile literature. | Olympics--Records. | African American women civil rights workers--Tennessee--Biography--Juvenile literature.
Classification: LCC GV1061.15.R83 M66 2025 (print) | LCC GV1061.15.R83 (ebook) | DDC 796.42092 [B]--dc23/eng/20231220
LC record available at https://lccn.loc.gov/2023054177
LC ebook record available at https://lccn.loc.gov/2023054178

Printed in the United States of America
Mankato, MN
082024

ABOUT THE AUTHOR

David Lee Morgan Jr. is the author of 11 books, including *LeBron James: The Rise of a Star* and *Breaking Through the Lines: The Marion Motley Story*. Morgan was a longtime sportswriter with the *Akron Beacon Journal* and is now a high school English teacher and public speaker.

TABLE OF CONTENTS

U.S.A
117
133

CHAPTER 1

THE FASTEST WOMAN

Wilma Rudolph needed just 11 seconds. That's about the amount of time it takes to tie both shoes. Rudolph used that time to become a champion. In 1960, she was taking part in the Olympic Games in Rome, Italy. She won a gold medal in the 100-meter race. Her time was 11.0 seconds.

Wilma Rudolph crosses the finish line to win the 100-meter race during the 1960 Olympic Games.

Rudolph launches off the starting blocks for the 200-meter race at the 1960 Olympics.

But that wasn't the only gold medal Rudolph won. She also ran the 200-meter race. She ran her first **heat** in 23.2 seconds. That broke the Olympic record. In the final, she started the race slow on the inside track. But she got faster and faster. Soon, she was far ahead of everyone else. She won gold with a time of 24.0 seconds.

Next, Rudolph ran in the 4x100-meter relay. She was the **anchor**. In the semifinals, her team recorded a time of 44.4 seconds. That set the world record.

TEAM PRIDE

Rudolph had much to be proud of at the 1960 Olympics. But she especially valued her relay team victory. She said standing on the award platform with her teammates meant the most. The four women had been teammates for years. All four attended college at Tennessee State University.

The team went on to win gold in the final. Rudolph became the first American woman to win three track-and-field gold medals in one Olympics.

It was also the first Summer Olympics on TV in the United States. As a result, millions of people saw Rudolph's spectacular performances. The media fell in love with her. People admired her graceful speed. She became an instant superstar. She received nicknames such as the "Black Gazelle" and the "Queen of the Olympics." She was also called the "Fastest Woman in the World." Rudolph was only 20 years old. But she had waited for this moment her whole life.

Rudolph stands on the podium with her gold medal for the 100-meter race.

Join
MARCH
OF
DIMES

CHAPTER 2

A WORLD OF BARRIERS

Wilma Rudolph was born on June 23, 1940, near Clarksville, Tennessee. She was often sick growing up. At age five, she contracted polio. The disease paralyzed her left leg. Wilma wore a leg brace to walk. She faced **discrimination** for her disability. Kids often teased her and left her out of activities.

Many kids with polio wore leg braces to help them walk.

Other barriers in the United States affected Wilma, too. Racist laws existed across the country. Some laws forced racial **segregation**. Some denied Black Americans the right to vote. Other laws prevented economic opportunities. In Southern states such as Tennessee, this system was called Jim Crow.

As a result, Wilma's family lived in a segregated part of Clarksville. They were poor. Wilma's large family helped care for her. They often massaged her leg.

There was a hospital near Wilma's home. But only white people could go there. The nearest Black hospital was in Nashville. That was more than 50 miles

Jim Crow laws racially segregated many public spaces, including drinking fountains.

(80 km) away. Every week, Wilma and her mother took the bus there. Black riders could not choose where they sat. If the bus was full, white riders took the seats. Black riders had to stand.

Even so, Wilma's treatment helped. By age 12, she could walk without a brace. She soon discovered that she loved sports.

At this point, Wilma faced yet another barrier. **Sexist** beliefs about female athletes were common. Many people did not think girls or women should take part in sports. For this reason, there were few athletic opportunities for girls.

However, Wilma thought those beliefs made no sense. And she wasn't afraid to be different from other girls. So, she practiced hard at the sports she loved.

This practice paid off quickly. She became a star at her segregated high school. In one basketball game, she scored 49 points. It set a state record.

Wilma was only 14 when Ed Temple noticed her. Temple was the women's

In 1952, Tennessee State sprinters Barbara Jones (middle left) and Mae Faggs (middle right) won Olympic gold.

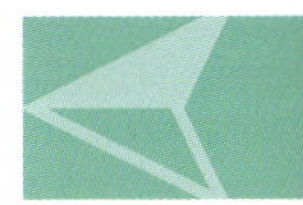

track-and-field coach for the Tennessee State Tigerbelles. Tennessee State was a historically Black college. Temple had turned the women's track-and-field team into a powerhouse. During summers, Wilma began training with the student athletes at Tennessee State.

U.S.
S.A.

CHAPTER 3

HOMETOWN HERO

Wilma Rudolph reached great heights while still in high school. In 1956, she competed in the Olympic Games in Melbourne, Australia. The 16-year-old was the youngest member of the US track-and-field team. However, going to the Games was costly. And Wilma's family still didn't have much money. But her

Margaret Matthews, Wilma Rudolph, Mae Faggs, and Isabelle Daniels won bronze in the 4x100-meter relay at the 1956 Olympics.

community in Clarksville helped. They pooled their money together to make sure Wilma could go.

Wilma didn't disappoint. She helped win a bronze medal in the 4x100-meter relay. But she wanted to do better. Her goal was to win gold at the 1960 Olympics.

In 1958, Rudolph began attending Tennessee State. As a Tigerbelle, she truly hit her stride. In 1960, she set the world record for the 200-meter race. She became the first woman to run it in less than 23 seconds.

At the 1960 Olympics, Rudolph's talent shone for the world to see. Her three gold

Rudolph waves to fans during her hometown parade in Clarksville, Tennessee.

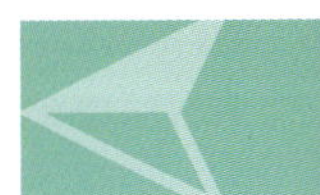

medals launched her into international stardom. She made TV appearances and received many honors.

Her hometown also wanted to hold a parade and dinner in Rudolph's honor. But leaders did not want it to be for all people. The governor wanted two celebrations.

He wanted one for white residents and one for Black residents.

Rudolph took a stand for the city's Black residents. She refused to take part if the event was segregated. The city changed its plans and agreed to Rudolph's wishes. It became the first **integrated** event in Clarksville's history.

PAVING THE WAY

Rudolph used her fame to increase opportunities for female athletes. After the 1960 Games, many invitation-only events wanted her to race. She was the first woman in years to be invited. Rudolph accepted only if she could race other women. As a result, the events began including women's events from then on.

President John F. Kennedy (left) meets with Rudolph at the White House in 1961.

Rudolph competed for a couple of years after 1960. She set a few more world records, too. But she retired from track in 1962. She was just 22 years old. At the time, track was an **amateur** sport. For this reason, Rudolph couldn't make a living from track.

CHAPTER 4

A BEAUTIFUL LIFE

By the early 1960s, the **civil rights movement** was gaining strength. It had been going on for years. Across the United States, Black Americans were pushing for their rights. One major demand was integration. And in 1963, this struggle hit Clarksville.

A white worker prevents a Black activist from sitting down at a segregated store in Memphis, Tennessee, in 1961.

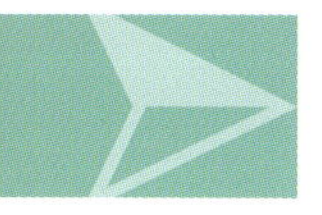

Rudolph tries to enter a segregated restaurant in Clarksville during a 1963 protest.

In 1963, one Clarksville restaurant wouldn't integrate. In response, 300 Black residents protested. Wilma Rudolph joined the protest. For two straight days, the group tried to eat at the restaurant. Both days, the white owners refused to let them in.

However, city leaders met. They said all restaurants should integrate. Soon after, the city voted. It decided to integrate all public places. Rudolph's action with a larger group had worked.

Afterward, Rudolph focused on her family and her career. She especially cared about sports and young people. She taught and coached. She also worked at community centers all over the United States.

Her **legacy** strengthened through the years. In 1973, she was voted into the Black Athletes Hall of Fame. The next year, she entered the National Track and Field Hall of Fame. Rudolph also kept her

Florence Griffith Joyner (left) meets with Rudolph in 1988.

connection to the Olympics. She joined the US Olympic Hall of Fame in 1983. She was also a TV commentator at the 1984 Olympics.

In July 1994, Rudolph learned she had cancer. The cancer quickly became worse.

Rudolph died on November 12. She was only 54 years old.

Rudolph faced discrimination because of her class, race, gender, and disability. Despite these barriers, she achieved many triumphs. She also worked to weaken those barriers for others.

THREE GENERATIONS

Wilma Rudolph helped pave the way for other Black female Olympians. Florence Griffith Joyner won three gold medals in the 1988 Olympics. She was the first woman to do that since Rudolph. In the 1980s and 1990s, Jackie Joyner-Kersee won six medals at four different Olympics. And at the 2012 Games, Allyson Felix won three golds. Felix said she was inspired by Rudolph, Griffith Joyner, and Joyner-Kersee.

WILMA RUDOLPH

- **Height:** 5 feet 11 inches (180 cm)
- **Weight:** 130 pounds (59 kg)
- **Born:** June 23, 1940
- **Died:** November 12, 1994
- **Birthplace:** Saint Bethlehem, Tennessee
- **High school:** Burt High School (Clarksville, Tennessee)
- **College:** Tennessee State University (Nashville, Tennessee) (1958–63)
- **Major achievements:** 4x100-meter relay Olympic bronze medal (1956); 100-meter Olympic gold medal (1960); 200-meter Olympic gold medal (1960); 4x100-meter relay Olympic gold medal (1960); Associated Press Woman Athlete of the Year (1960, 1961); National Track and Field Hall of Fame (1974); US Olympic Hall of Fame (1983)

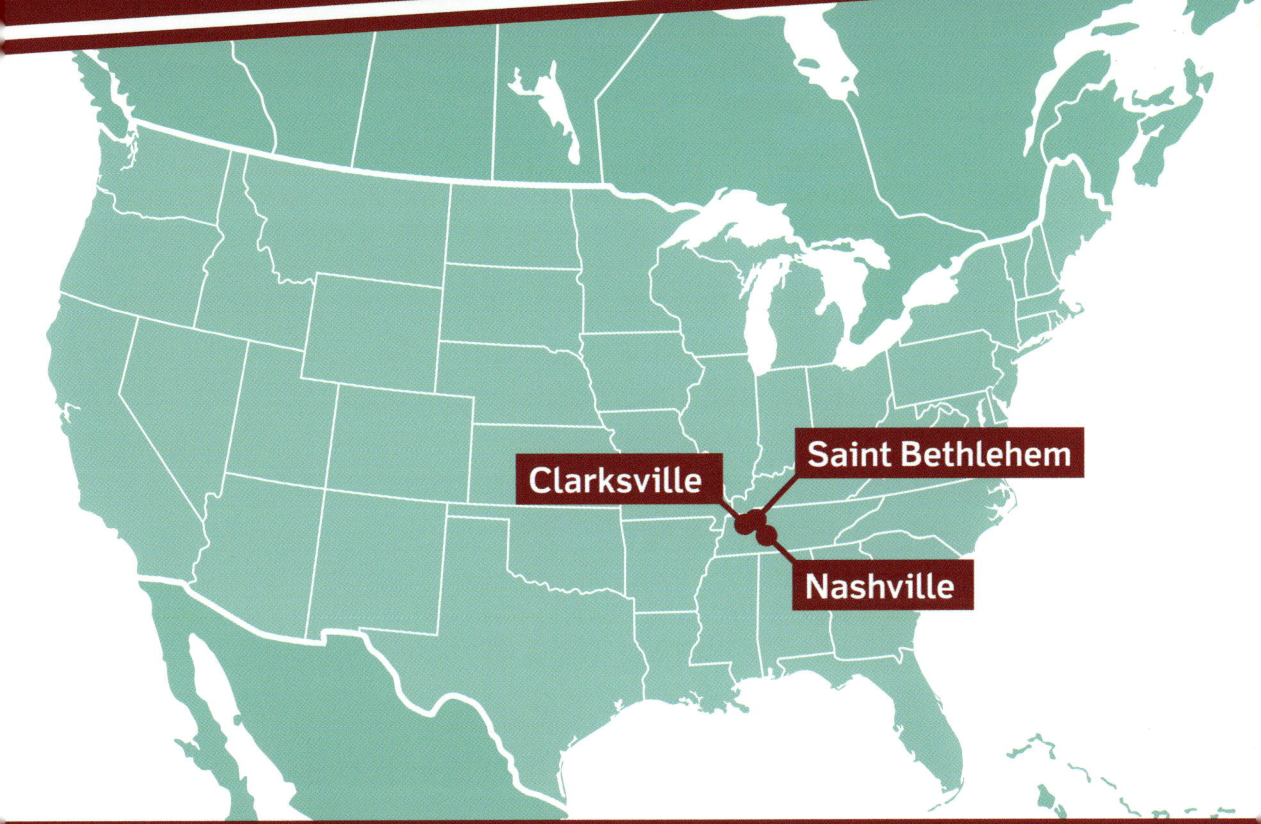
Saint Bethlehem
Clarksville
Nashville

Rome

Melbourne

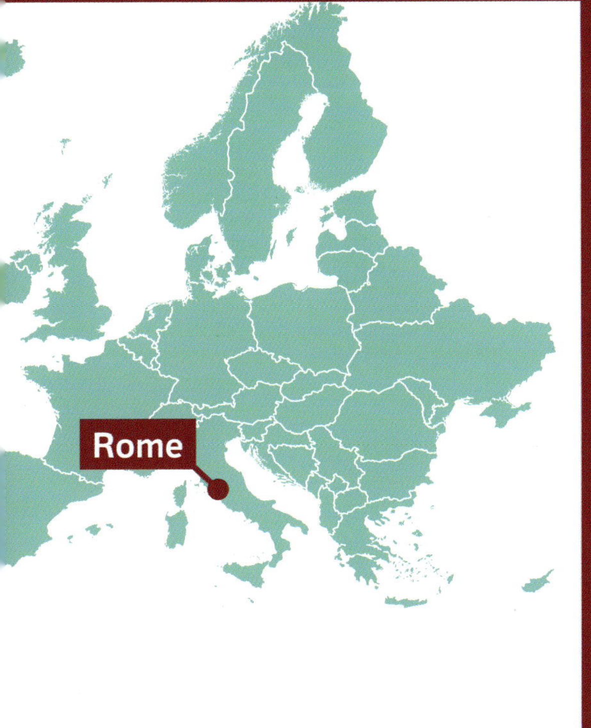

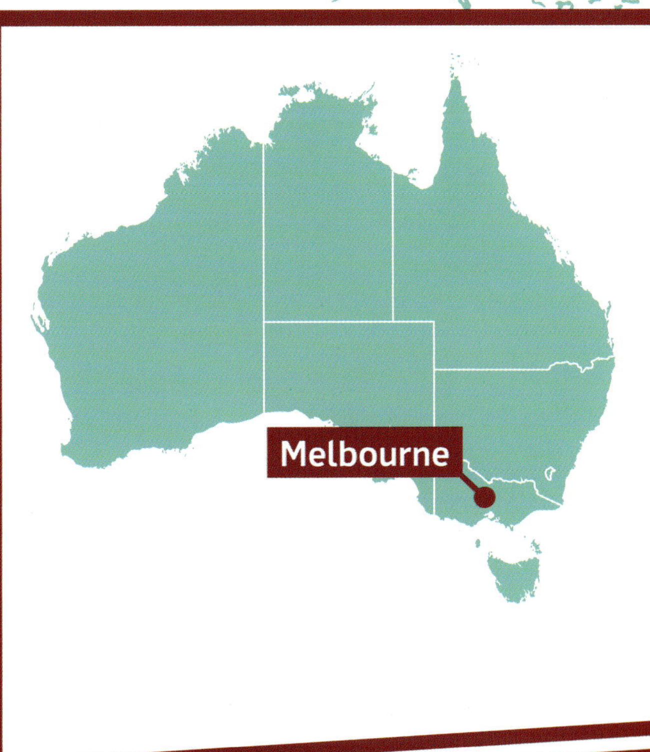

FOCUS ON
WILMA RUDOLPH

Write your answers on a separate piece of paper.

1. Write a paragraph describing the barriers Wilma Rudolph faced during her childhood.
2. What are some similarities between the 1960 Clarksville parade and the 1963 Clarksville protest? What are some differences?
3. When did Rudolph compete in the Olympics for the first time?
   - **A.** 1956
   - **B.** 1960
   - **C.** 1988
4. How did TV help make Rudolph such a huge star?
   - **A.** More people could see Rudolph's talent as it happened.
   - **B.** Fewer people learned about Rudolph's gold medals.
   - **C.** TV stations helped Rudolph prepare for her races.

Answer key on page 32.

GLOSSARY

amateur
Someone who is not paid to perform an activity.

anchor
An athlete who runs the last leg of a relay race.

civil rights movement
A mass struggle against racial discrimination in the United States in the 1950s and 1960s.

discrimination
Unfair treatment of others based on who they are or how they look.

heat
An early round of a competition.

integrated
Including people of different races.

legacy
The things a person becomes known for.

segregation
The separation of groups of people based on race or other factors.

sexist
Having to do with hatred or mistreatment of people because of their gender.

TO LEARN MORE

BOOKS

Bowman, Chris. *Going for Gold: Wilma Rudolph and the 1960 Olympics*. Minneapolis: Bellwether Media, 2024.

Leed, Percy. *Wilma Rudolph: Running for Gold.* Minneapolis: Lerner Publications, 2021.

Rosen, Karen. *Trailblazing Women in Track and Field.* Chicago: Norwood House Press, 2023.

NOTE TO EDUCATORS

Visit **www.focusreaders.com** to find lesson plans, activities, links, and other resources related to this title.

INDEX

Answer Key: 1. Answers will vary; **2.** Answers will vary; **3.** A; **4.** A